EXPLORING JAZZ

SCALES FOR KEYBOARD

by Bill Boyd

ISBN 0-7935-1544-0

HAL•LEONARD®
CORPORATION
7777 W. BLUEMOUND RD. P.O. BOX 13819 MILWAUKEE, WI 53213

FOREWORD

Scales provide the basis for jazz improvisation and fill-ins. The scales presented in this book produce idiomatic sounds associated with many jazz styles. The "jazz scales" may be simply defined as those which do not fall into the traditional category.

This book explores the jazz scales and examines their potential. While this is not a jazz improvisation method, the study of the material will certainly provide the player with additional resources in this area.

A knowledge of chords and chord construction is helpful to fully benefit from this book.

Each chapter includes charts with the scales written in all keys with suggested fingerings and a list of chords which complement each scale. Music examples apply the scales to jazz chord progressions and compositions.

Upon completion of this volume, the keyboard player will gain new insights into the practical application of the jazz scales and enhance performance.

CONTENTS

1: FUNCTION OF CHORDS

The jazz scales presented in this book provide the basis for improvised jazz lines or short fill-ins and endings. An improvised jazz line is an original melodic invention which lasts for the length of a jazz tune. Short fill-ins are melodic fragments which are added when the melody pauses for a brief time (four to eight beats). Endings are one or two measure ideas at the conclusion of a song.

In order to determine which scale is appropriate for a particular chord, it is necessary to know where the chord appears within the context of a chord progression. In other words, realize how the chord FUNCTIONS within the chord progression.

The function of chords is best described in terms of Roman Numerals. The scale tones in a given key are numbered from one to seven. The first note of the scale is called the TONIC (or 1). It is the note for which the scale is named.

C MAJOR SCALE:

Chords built on these scale tones are labeled with Roman Numerals which correspond to the scale steps. The note in the scale upon which the chord is constructed is called the chord ROOT. The root of the chord is the note for which the chord is named. The letter name of the chord is the same as the chord root.

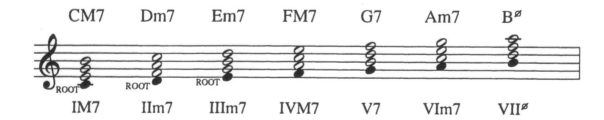

The chord type (major, minor, dom. 7th) at any level of the scale may vary. The F major seventh chord in the last example could be a dominant seventh or minor seventh, etc.

To select a scale which would complement a G7 chord, it is necessary to determine the function of the chord within the context of a chord progression. For example, the G7 chord functions as a V7 in the key of C, a VI7 in the key of B♭, a II7 in the key of F, a III7 in the key of E♭ and as a VII7 in the key of A♭.

Each function of the G7 chord might require a different scale. The scale which complements a G7 chord in the key of C may not work with a G7 chord in the key of E♭.

Many jazz tunes change keys within the composition. Key changes are established by the presence of V7 I or IIm7 V7 I. I chords, which are always some type of major chord (in a major key), are called the TONIC or KEY CHORD. Not all major chords are tonic chords but if they are preceded by IIm7 V7, a new key is established. The I chord in a minor key is minor or minor sixth. When a key change occurs the Roman numerals must be adjusted in terms of the new key.

Sometimes just the presence of a IIm7 V7 is enough to establish a new key momentarily. This is more difficult to analyze because the key chord is not present.

In the following example the final C chord is the only KEY CHORD as it is preceded by a V7. Even though the other chords are major, there is no key change because the IIm7 V7 I progression is not established.

CHORD SYMBOLS

MAJOR	letter alone (C) M7 maj7 Δ	major triad major 7th chord
MINOR	m or - m7 -7	minor triad minor seventh
DOMINANT 7th	7	dominant 7th chord
DIMINISHED	o or dim.	diminished 7th
HALF DIMINISHED	ø same as m7♭5	half diminished 7th

SYMBOLS FOR ALTERED CHORDS: ♭ or - = flatted...lowered

♯ or + = augmented...raised...sharped

MUSIC EXAMPLES

The music examples in each chapter are notated with no key signatures. All accidentals are written in. The eighth notes are to be played according to the style of the music.

SWING	uneven eighth notes	♫ = ♪♪ (triplet)
ROCK	even eighth notes	♫ = ♫
SLOW/DRILLS	even eighth notes	♫ = ♫

As the tempo increases in swing style the eighth notes are played more evenly.

2: THE MAJOR PENTATONIC SCALE

The Major Pentatonic Scale contains five notes from the major scale. To construct this scale in any key, extract the tonic (first), second, third, fifth and sixth notes from the major scale.

C MAJOR SCALE: Bb MAJOR SCALE:

The FORMULA for constructing a major pentatonic scale in any key is:

1 2 3 5 6 of any major scale.

C MAJOR PENTATONIC SCALE:

APPLICATIONS:	Limited for improvisation. Good for short fill-ins and endings.	
CHORDS:	6/9, M7, M7#11 7, 9, 13, 7sus m9	

RESTRICTIONS:	Not to be used with:
	    altered dominant 7th chords
	    dom. 7th chords functioning as III7, VI7 or VII7
	    V7 in minor keys	

The scales discussed in this chapter are: C, F, G, E, Bb, Eb, Ab and D. *Be aware of the various styles of music each exercise represents.* All scales appear at the end of this chapter with suggested fingerings. The chords for each scale are written underneath.

The following examples illustrate the C major pentatonic scale as an ending for a slow ballad. Always play the scales with the suggested fingerings.

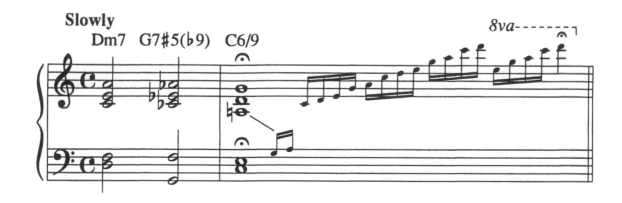

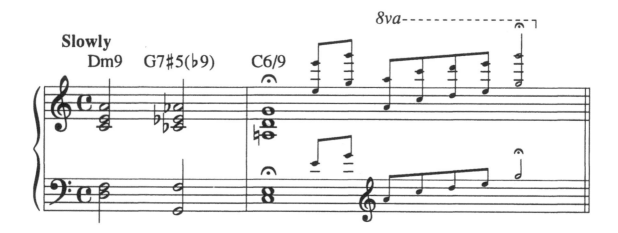

Throughout this book the choice of scale often depends upon which chord tones are to be emphasized. The C major pentatonic scale emphasizes the 6th and 9th in the examples above. The same scale emphasizes the major 7th (along with the 6th and 9th) in the F major chord. The next example is an ending to a slow ballad in the key of F major.

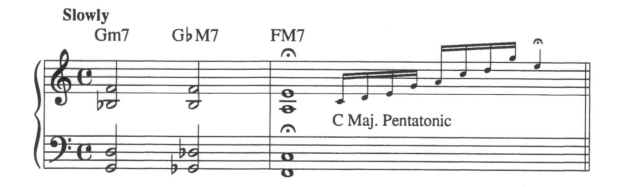

The major pentatonic scale may emphasize the major 7th and the #11. In the next example the #11 (+11) is emphasized on the Db chord. The #11 is notated as a G natural in this scale.

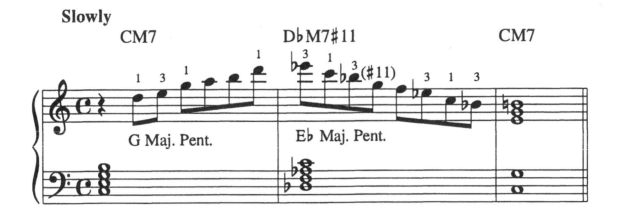

The #11 emphasized in an ending:

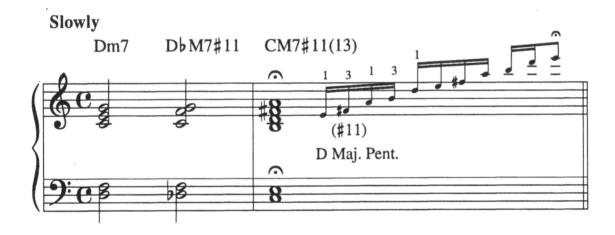

Emphasizing the 4th in a dom.7 sus. chord. (The chord contains no 3rd.)

The 6 and 9 emphasized in an ending...moderate tempo, steady beat.

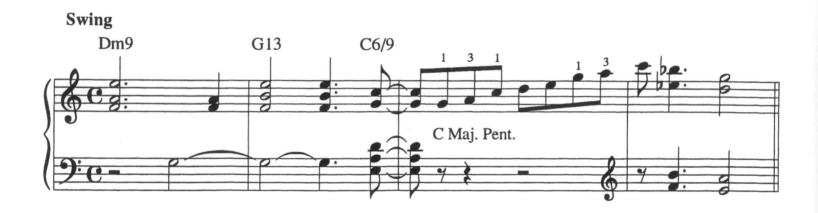

Below is a progression of dominant 9th chords. The scales emphasize the 9th and 13th.

Emphasizing the 9th in the m9 chord:

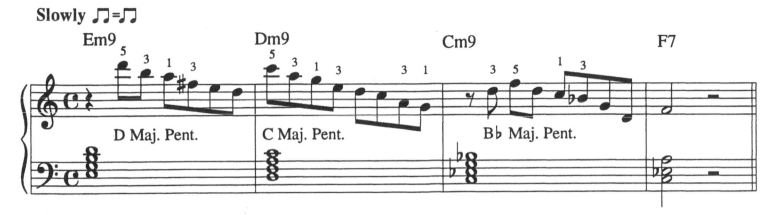

The melody below has several pauses where fill-ins may be inserted.

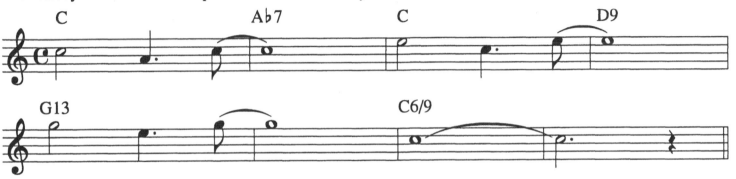

Fill-ins replace the long notes:

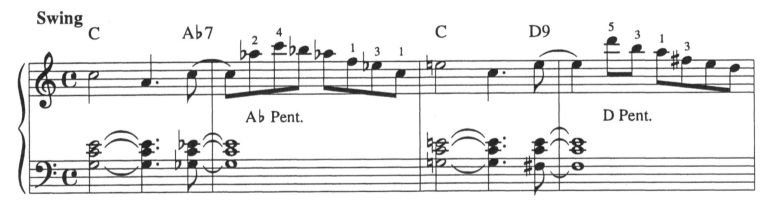

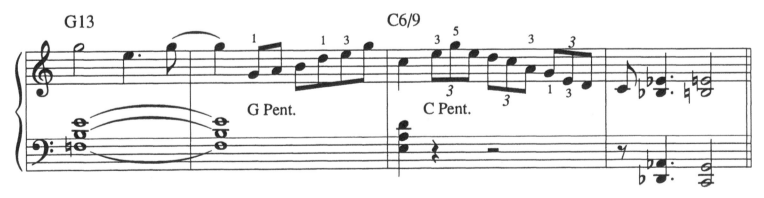

The scales may begin on notes other than the tonic and proceed in any direction.

The following pages contain the major pentatonic scales in all keys. It is important to follow the suggested fingerings. Memorize the chords which complement each scale. Practice starting the scales on notes other than the tonic. Play the scale through the entire range of the keyboard.

MAJOR PENTATONIC SCALES IN ALL KEYS

C

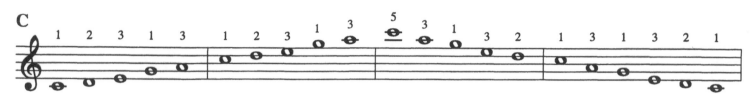

CHORDS: C6/9, D7sus, C9, FM7, Dm9, B♭M7#11

F

CHORDS: F6/9, G7sus, F9, B♭M7, Gm9, E♭M7#11

B♭

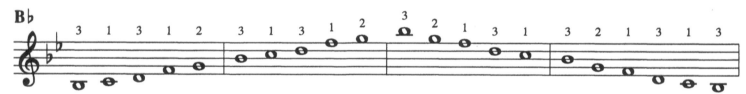

CHORDS: B♭6/9, C7sus, B♭9, E♭M7, Cm9, A♭M7#11

E♭

CHORDS: E♭6/9, F7sus, E♭9, A♭M7, Fm9, D♭M7#11

A♭

CHORDS: A♭6/9, B♭7sus, A♭9, D♭M7, B♭m9, G♭M7#11

D♭

CHORDS: D♭6/9, E♭7sus, D♭9, G♭M7, E♭m9, BM7#11

Gb

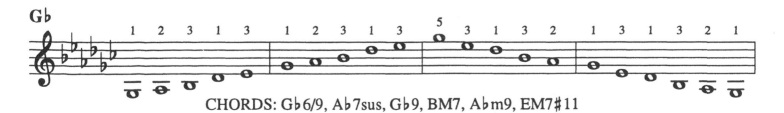

CHORDS: Gb6/9, Ab7sus, Gb9, BM7, Abm9, EM7#11

B

CHORDS: B6/9, Db7sus, B9, EM7, Dbm9, AM7#11

E

CHORDS: E6/9, Gb7sus, E9, AM7, Gbm9, DM7#11

A

CHORDS: A6/9, B7sus, A9, DM7, Bm9, GM7#11

D

CHORDS: D6/9, E7sus, B9, GM7, Em9, CM7#11

G

CHORDS: G6/9, A7sus, G9, CM7, Am9, FM7#11

3: THE RELATIVE MINOR PENTATONIC SCALE

The relative minor and the major pentatonic scales have the same relationship to one another as the relative minor and major scales have in traditional harmony. Both scales contain the SAME NOTES...only the TONIC shifts. The tonic of the minor pentatonic scale is a minor third below the tonic of the major scale.

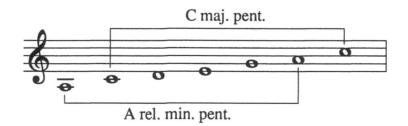

C maj. pent.

A rel. min. pent.

Most authorities refer to this scale as the minor pentatonic. The word "relative" is used here to emphasize the relationship to the major pentatonic. The fingerings are the same with few exceptions. These scales appear at the end of this chapter in all keys with fingerings and the chords written underneath.

FORMULA: 1 ♭3 4 5 ♭7 of any major scale.

A MAJOR SCALE: A MINOR PENTATONIC SCALE:

In the above example a natural sign is necessary to flat a sharped note. The minor pentatonic scales are notated in the minor key signatures for ease of reading.

A MINOR PENTATONIC SCALE:

APPLICATIONS:	Good for short improvisations in a minor key. Short fill-ins.
CHORDS:	minor, m7, m11 Dom. 7th functioning as V7 in minor.
RESTRICTIONS:	Limited with V7 in minor.

The minor pentatonic scale will complement a m7 or m11 chord regardless of function. It will only complement a dominant 7th chord when the chord functions as a V7 in a minor key. A further discussion of this chord/scale relationship in minor keys appears in Chapter 8.

The following example illustrates the F minor pentatonic scale in a slow ad-lib tempo ballad. The ending is a variation on the E♭ major pentatonic. The scale is played in both hands at different levels.

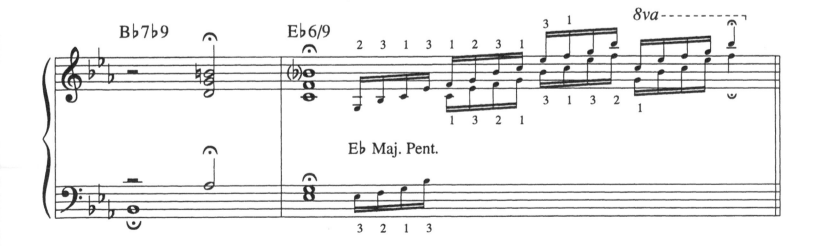

The next three examples apply the appropriate minor pentatonic scale to minor seventh chords.

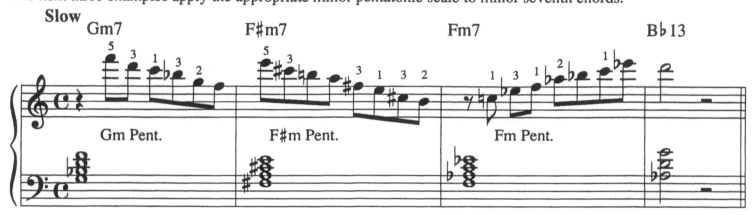

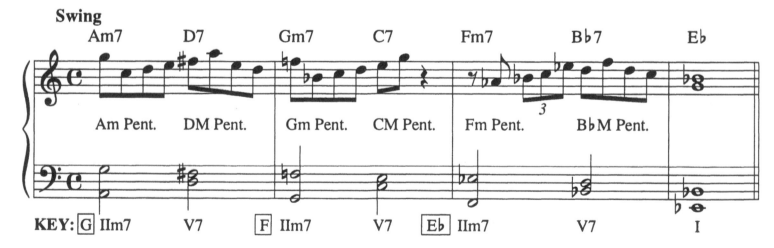

The minor pentatonic is effective for improvised jazz solos in minor keys. (More about this in Chapter 8.)

KEY OF F MINOR:

A double note device produces a "funky" sound with the minor pentatonic scale. The scale notes or melody notes are on the bottom and the top note remains stationary. Two positions are necessary in order to include all scale tones. One position has the tonic as the top note and the other position has the fourth note of the minor pentatonic scale as the top note.

A MINOR PENTATONIC

A three measure jazz phrase with this double note device:

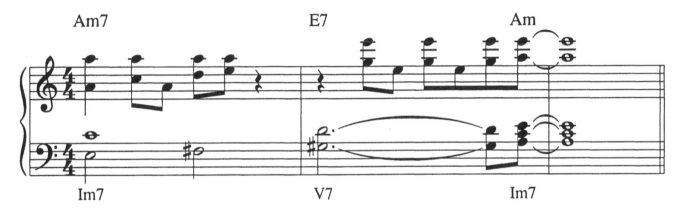

PLAYING FROM A FAKE BOOK

Fake books do not always indicate four note chords. Major triads should be played as major 7th or 6/9 and minor chords are changed to m7 with or without added notes. Dominant 7th chords with altered notes are not possible now. Altered dominant 7th chords and their corresponding scales are discussed in Chapter 5.

Select a song from a FAKE book. Analyze the chords in terms of their function. Look for the KEY CHORDS and possible key changes. Adjust the Roman numerals in terms of the new key. Look on the scale charts to see which scales complement a particular chord. If a dominant 7th chord functions as a III7, VI7 or VII7 it is not possible to play a pentatonic scale at this time.

Below is a chord progression which is often played by jazz musicians. This progression changes keys every four measures.

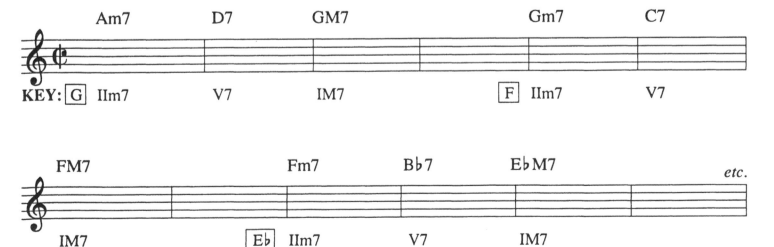

The improvisation on this chord progression is based solely on major and minor pentatonic scales. In the original song all of the dominant 7th chords are altered. In this example the V chords are unaltered dominant sevenths. The added color of the altered chords is missed in this version.

The above improvisation may sound somewhat contrived and uninteresting. The exclusive use of pentatonic scales along with the absence of the altered dominant sevenths cause this effect. A good jazz improvisation also includes the traditional major and minor scales, modal scales and arpeggios. The examples in this book will over-use a particular scale when it is the subject of a chapter. It is the skillful application of all the improvisational melodic devices which produces a good jazz line.

(RELATIVE) MINOR PENTATONIC SCALES

Am

CHORDS: Am7, Am11, E7 (V7 in min.), Am

Dm

CHORDS: Dm7, Dm11, A7 (V7 in min.), Dm

Gm

CHORDS: Gm7, Gm11, D7 (V7 in min.), Gm

Cm

CHORDS: Cm7, Cm11, G7 (V7 in min.), Cm

Fm

CHORDS: Fm7, Fm11, C7 (V7 in min.), Fm

B♭m

CHORDS: B♭m7, B♭m11, F7 (V7 in min.), B♭m

20

E♭m

CHORDS: E♭m7, E♭m11, B♭7 (V7 in min.), E♭m

(A♭m)
G♯m

CHORDS: A♭m7, A♭m11, E♭7 (V7 in min.), A♭m

(D♭m)
C♯m

CHORDS: D♭m7, D♭m11, A♭7 (V7 in min.), D♭m

(G♭m)
F♯m

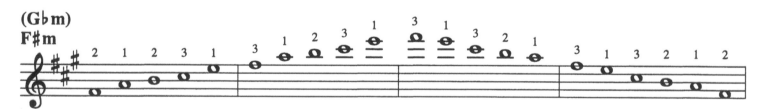

CHORDS: G♭m7, G♭m11, D♭7 (V7 in min.), G♭m

Bm

CHORDS: Bm7, Bm11, F♯7 (V7 in minor), Bm

Em

CHORDS: Em7, Em11, B7 (V7 in min.), Em

4: THE MAJOR PENTATONIC SCALE (add ♭7)

The seventh from the major scale is flatted and added to the major pentatonic scale.

FORMULA: 1 2 3 5 6 ♭7 of any major scale

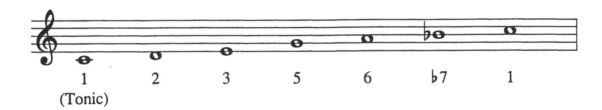

1   2   3   5   6   ♭7   1
(Tonic)

This scale in all keys with fingerings and chords appears at the end of this chapter.

C MAJOR PENTATONIC SCALE (add ♭7)

APPLICATIONS:	Slow and fast fill-ins Some limited improvisation
CHORDS:	Dominant 7th 9th 13th m7♭5 or ∅
RESTRICTIONS:	Not good with: 　　　dom. 7th chords functioning as 　　　III7 VI7 VII7 or altered dom. 7ths 　　　V7 in minor key

Memorize the C, F, B♭ and E♭ major pentatonic scales with ♭7.

22

The following exercise is an excellent model for the practice of all scales. In practical playing the scales do not always begin or end with the tonic. Notice that the next scale begins where the last one ended. The smooth connection from one scale to another is important for improvisation.

DRILL FOR MAJOR PENTATONIC SCALE add ♭7:

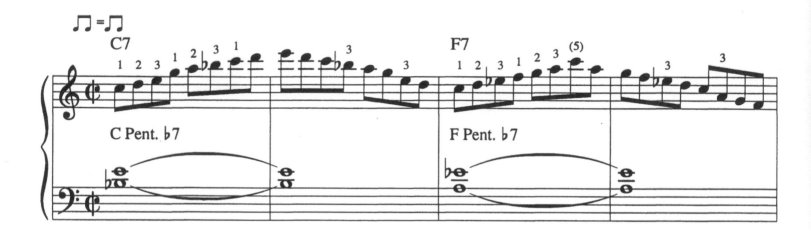

Dominant 7th chords often progress downward in half steps. It is not necessary that all notes of the scale be present in a fill-in or improvisation. Measure one below is an incomplete scale.

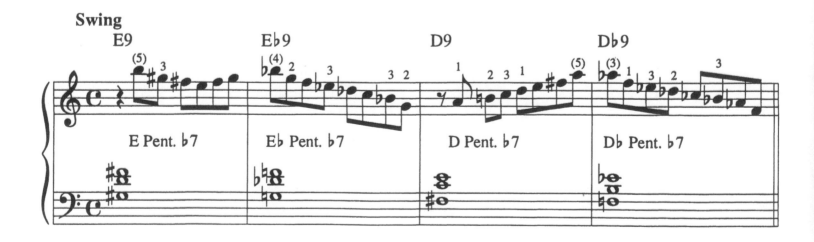

Very often the dominant 7th chord whose root is one half step above the tonic chord replaces the V7 chord...♭II7 IM7. The progression is usually IIm7 ♭II7 IM7 instead of IIm7 V7 IM7.

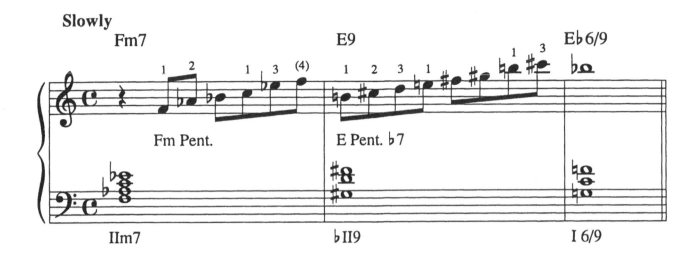

This replacement device or substitution (as it is more often called) is also possible in minor keys. The chord progression below is Im ♭II7 Im instead of Im V7 Im. The ♭II7 SUBSTITUTES for the V7 chord.

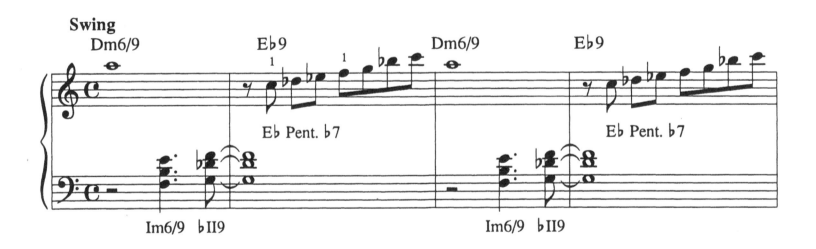

The II chord in a minor key is a minor seventh with the flatted 5th (m7♭5). This chord is sometimes analyzed as a half diminished seventh chord. Both chords are the same and are interchangeable. The chord symbol for the half diminished 7th is: ∅.

Below the major pentatonic scale with the ♭7 is applied to the II chord in the key of D minor.

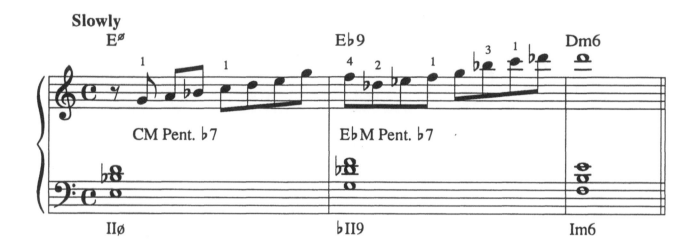

The last example illustrates the more traditional II∅ V7 Im chord progression. The major pentatonic with the ♭7 is applied to the II chord. In this style the minor pentatonic scale suggested for the V7 chord in the previous chapter is inappropriate. Chapter 5 will deal with this chord progression and a thorough discussion of minor key scale/chord relationships appears in Chapter 8.

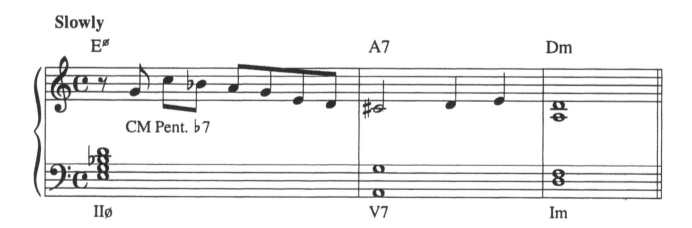

Return to the fake book and apply the scales to some songs. Experiment with minor keys.

MAJOR PENTATONIC SCALES (add ♭7)

C

CHORDS: C9, C13, E∅

F

CHORDS: F9, F13, A∅

B♭

CHORDS: B♭9, B♭13, D∅

E♭

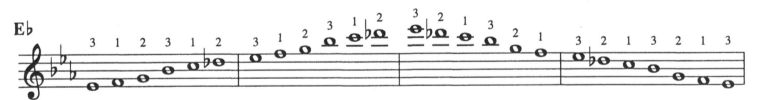

CHORDS: E♭9, E♭13, G∅

A♭

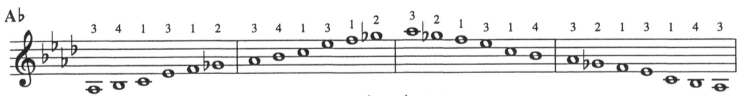

CHORDS: A♭9, A♭13, C∅

D♭

CHORDS: D♭9, D♭13, F∅

G♭

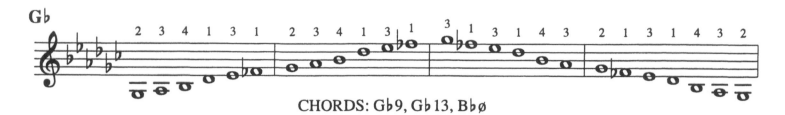

CHORDS: G♭9, G♭13, B♭ø

B

CHORDS: B9, B13, E♭ø

E

CHORDS: E9, E13, A♭ø

A

CHORDS: A9, A13, D♭ø

D

CHORDS: D9, D13, G♭ø

G

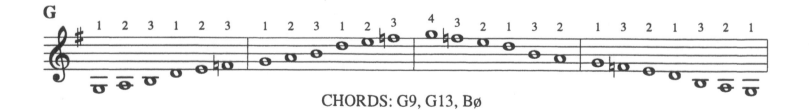

CHORDS: G9, G13, Bø

5: PARALLEL MINOR PENTATONIC SCALE

The parallel minor pentatonic scale and the major pentatonic scale share the same tonic. The notes of the two scales are identical with the exception of the third step of the major scale, which is flatted.

MAJOR PENTATONIC SCALE

PARALLEL MINOR PENTATONIC SCALE

The formula for the construction of this scale in any key:

1 2 ♭3 5 6 of any major scale.

C PARALLEL MINOR PENTATONIC SCALE:

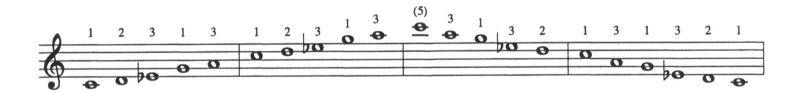

This scale appears in all keys with fingerings and chords at the end of the chapter.

APPLICATIONS:	Endings in minor keys.
	Short fill-ins major and minor keys.
	Beginning blues improvisation.
	Short blues riffs.
CHORDS:	m6, ⦰, 7, 9, 13, 7♭9, 7#5(♭9)(#9), M7#11

The parallel minor pentatonic scale is the most versatile of the scales studied thus far. Its ambiguity allows it to complement many different harmonic situations.

The parallel minor pentatonic scale (abbr. P/m pent.) will complement three types of dominant 7th chords. Scale selection depends upon which notes of the chord are to be emphasized. The C7 chord will serve as a model.

Chord	Scale	Notes emphasized
C7	G P/m	9th and 13th
C7	B♭ P/m	♭9th
C7	D♭ P/m	#5, ♭9, #9

The exercises below utilize these scale/chord relationships.

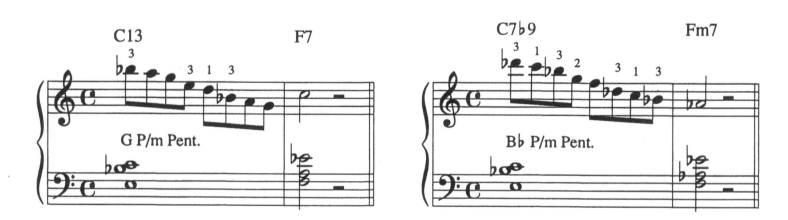

The scales which emphasize the altered notes in the chord will complement the V7 chord in minor keys. They work equally well with the V7 in major keys. The scale which emphasizes the ♭9 will complement the III7, VI7 and VII7 chords in most instances. These chords are often preceded by m7 chords and a temporary II V relationship is established.

The next example illustrates this progression. The key is E♭ major. The D7 and C7 chords are VII7 and VI7 chords in this key. Since they are preceded by m7 chords the progression is analyzed as a temporary key change. The scale choice for these chords emphasizes the ♭9. In the second to last measure the scale choice emphasizes the #5, ♭9 and #9.

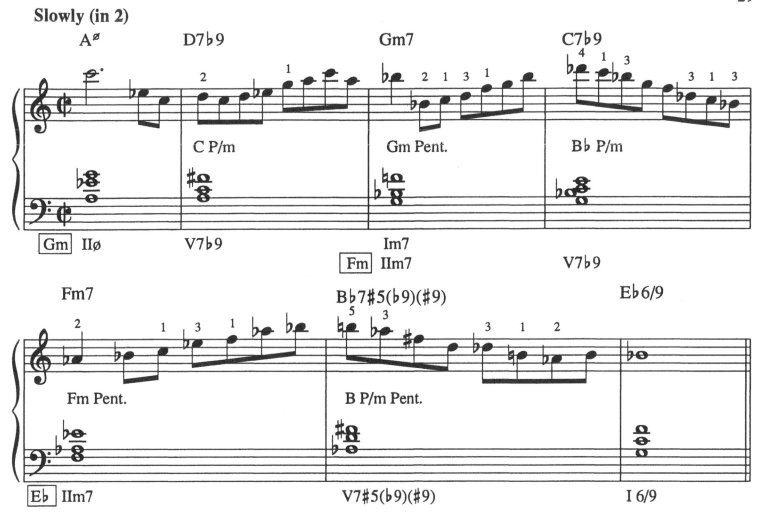

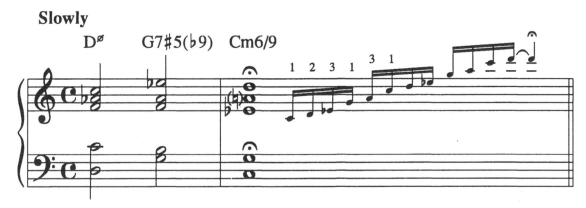

The C P/m pentatonic as an ending for a slow ballad in the key of C minor:

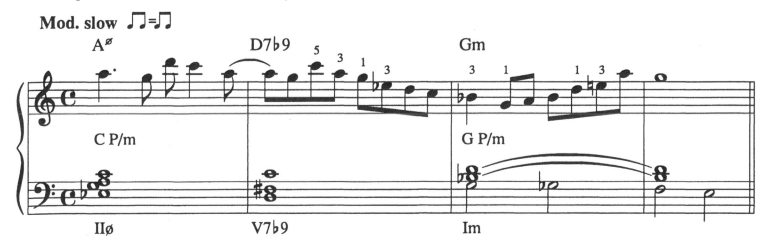

The P/m pent. for IIø V7♭9 Im in the key of G minor:

The next example is I II V I in the key of C minor. All notes are from the P/m pent. scales. The third measure from the end substitutes the ♭II7 for the V7 chord.

The P/m pentatonic scale may be applied to the major 7 with the #11 (+11).

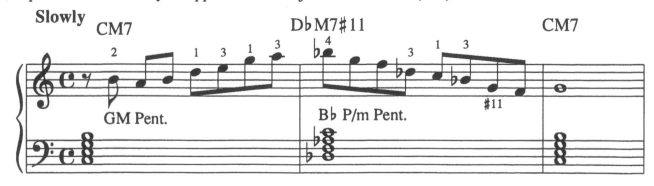

The IV chord in a major key is sometimes m6. The example below applies the C P/m pent. scale to the IV minor chord.

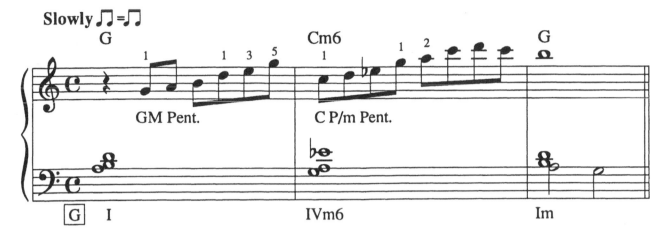

A dominant 9th chord whose root is a perfect fourth above the IVm often substitutes for the IV minor chord. Below the F9 substitutes for the Cm6 in the key of G major.

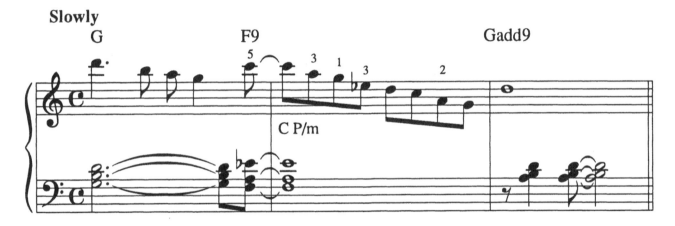

The next example is a series of dominant 9th and 13th chords with the P/m pent. scale.

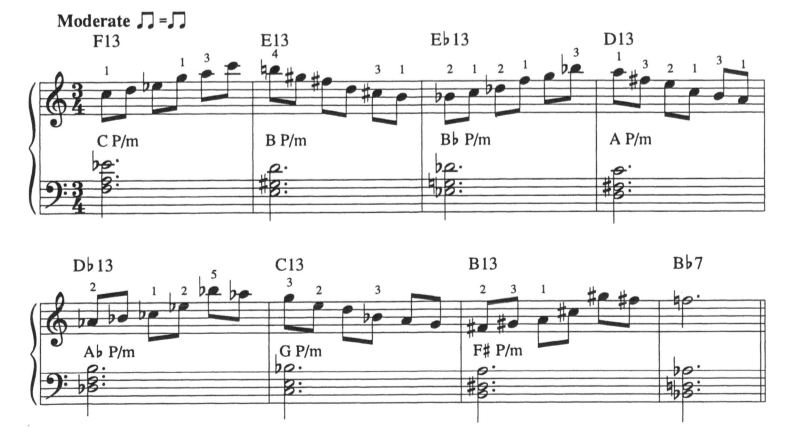

BASIC BLUES IMPROVISATION

The most surprising application of the P/m pent. scale is to the blues. The blues sound is produced by playing notes borrowed from minor keys in the right hand while playing major key harmony in the left hand. The notes of this scale fit the three chords (I IV7 V7) which are used to harmonize the basic blues. Think of three lines of four measures each.

BASIC BLUES CHORD PROGRESSION

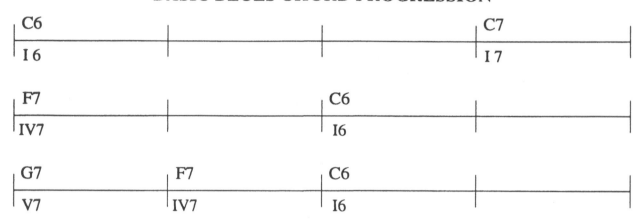

The parallel minor pent. scale when applied to blues produces a sound which is characteristic of 40's swing and 50's rock. The first example is rock (even eighth notes). The notes of the C parallel minor pentatonic scale are played throughout the twelve measures.

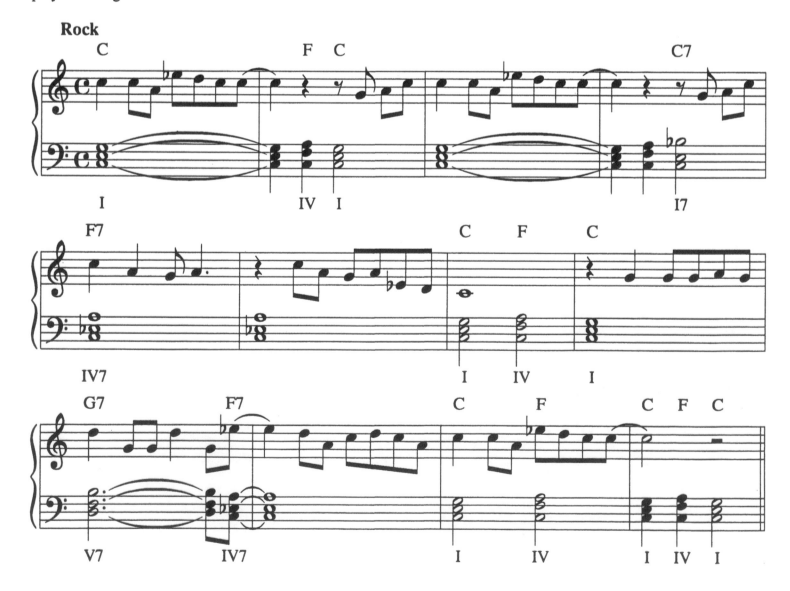

RIFFS

Many jazz tunes of the 40's used riffs. A riff is a short melodic idea which is repeated. Below is a four measure riff based upon the notes of the C parallel minor pentatonic scale. Play the four measures three times in order to extend the riff into a twelve measure blues melody. The left hand may play the blues chords. The eighth notes are to be played unevenly (swing style).

RIFF

Left hand chords:

Invent some four measure riffs with the notes from the C P/m pentatonic scale and extend them to twelve measures.

The next example is a twelve measure blues improvisation. Play the chords indicated above the staff with the left hand. The eighth notes are swing style.

Improvise a twelve measure blues with the notes of the C P/m pentatonic scale.

34

It is important to restate the fact that in practical playing no scale is used exclusively. There are other options for blues improvisation.

SUMMARY OF PENTATONIC SCALE USE*

CHORDS	SCALES			
	MAJOR PENT.	MINOR PENT.	MAJOR PENT. ♭7	PARALLEL MINOR
6/9, M7	●			
M7♯11	●			●
m7, m11		●		
m9	●			
∅			●	●
m6				●
dom.7 9-13	●		●	●
7♭9				●
7♭9 ♯5 ♯9				●
V7 (natural minor)		●		●
7sus	●			

*Application to blues summarized in a later chapter.

To find a specific scale for a specific chord check the scale charts at the end of each chapter.

PARALLEL MINOR PENTATONIC SCALES

Cm

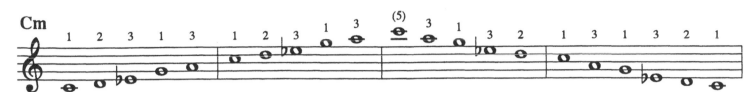

CHORDS: E♭M7#11, Cm6, Aø, F13, D7♭9, B7#5(♭9)(#9), (C blues)

Fm

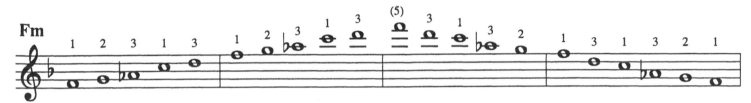

CHORDS: A♭M7#11, Fm6, Dø, B♭13, G7♭9, E7#5(♭9)(#9), (F blues)

B♭m

CHORDS: D♭M7#11, B♭m6, Gø, E♭13, C7♭9, A7#5(♭9)(#9), (B♭ blues)

E♭m

CHORDS: G♭M7#11, E♭m6, Cø, A♭13, F7♭9, D7#5(♭9)(#9), (E♭ blues)

A♭m

CHORDS: BM7#11, A♭m6, Fø, D♭13, B♭7♭9, G7#5(♭9)(#9), (A♭ blues)

D♭m

CHORDS: EM7#11, D♭m6, B♭ø, G♭13, E♭7♭9, C7#5(♭9)(#9), (D♭ blues)

G♭m

CHORDS: AM7#11, G♭m6, E♭ø, B13, A♭7♭9, F7#5(♭9)(#9), (G♭ blues)

Bm

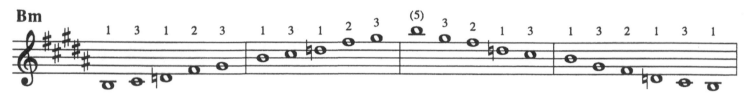

CHORDS: DM7#11, Bm6, A♭ø, E13, D♭7♭9, B♭7#5(♭9)(#9), (B blues)

Em

CHORDS: GM7#11, Em6, D♭ø, A13, G♭7♭9, E♭7#5(♭9)(#9), (E blues)

Am

CHORDS: CM7#11, Am6, F#ø, D13, B7♭9, A♭7#5(♭9)(#9), (A blues)

Dm

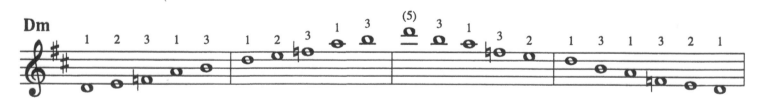

CHORDS: FM7#11, Dm6, Bø, G13, E7♭9, D♭7#5(♭9)(#9), (D blues)

Gm

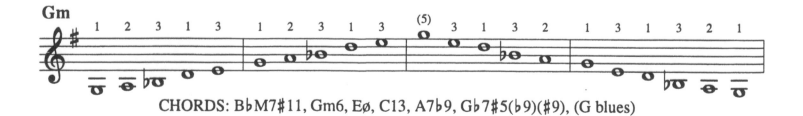

CHORDS: B♭M7#11, Gm6, Eø, C13, A7♭9, G♭7#5(♭9)(#9), (G blues)

6: THE MAJOR BLUES SCALE

FORMULA: 1 2 ♭3(♯2) 3 5 6 of any major scale.

C MAJOR SCALE

Tonic 2 3 4 5 6 7 1

C MAJOR BLUES SCALE

Tonic 2 ♭3 ♮3 5 6 1

The ♭3 is notated as a ♯2 in ascending passages and as a ♭3 in descending passages. The major blues scales in all keys appear at the end of the chapter.

C MAJOR BLUES SCALE:

Fingering:

APPLICATIONS:	Swing and rock of 40's and 50's
	Dixieland jazz
	Improvisation on swing tunes and blues
	Fast or slow fill-ins
	Endings on swing tunes and blues
CHORDS:	6/9, Dom. 7 9 13
RESTRICTIONS:	Not to be used with:
	altered dom. 7th chords
	dom. 7th functioning as VII7,
	III7 or VI7
	V7 in minor keys

The major blues scale produces a "bluesy" sound which is characteristic of swing and rock styles of the 40's and 50's. It is also applied to Dixieland and blues. Careful listening to jazz recordings will reveal that this scale is also heard in jazz styles of later periods.

38

The ♭3 is the note which produces the bluesy effect. In ascending scale passages the #2 is heard as a passing tone between 2 and 3. In the descending scale the ♭3 is heard as a blues note.

Ascending   Descending

The blues sound is emphasized when the natural 3 is omitted from the phrase and the ♭3 is played exclusively. In the following examples A and B are similar phrases only B emphasizes the ♭3. The same is true of C and D.

The exercise below is a series of dominant seventh chords. In each measure the ♭3 is emphasized to produce a bluesy feeling.

In the next series of chromatic dominant seventh chords the ♭3 is not emphasized until the last measure.

Fill-ins with the major blues scale:

Below are two four measure endings with the notes of the C major blues scale.

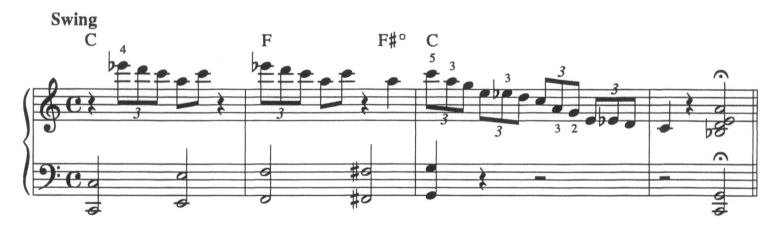

A typical 50's chord progression is I VIm7 IIm7 V7. The major blues scale may complement each of the chords but only in the context of this progression.

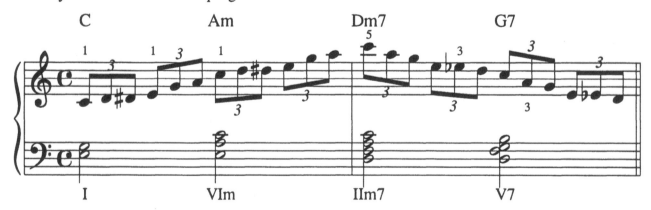

In terms of the key of C in the example below: The C major blues scale would normally not complement the Am7, Dm7 and G7 chords. Therefore these chords do not appear on the scale chart at the end of the chapter.

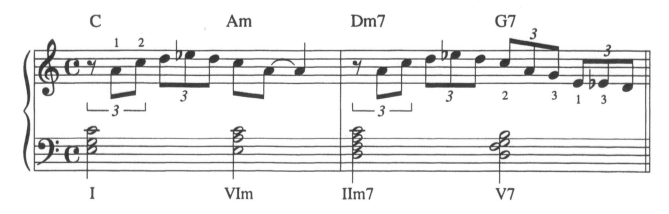

The same is true for the II7 chord. In the following examples the D7 chord appears with the C major blues scale. In this context it works...but the D7 chord is more often used with the D major blues scale or some appropriate scale from another chapter.

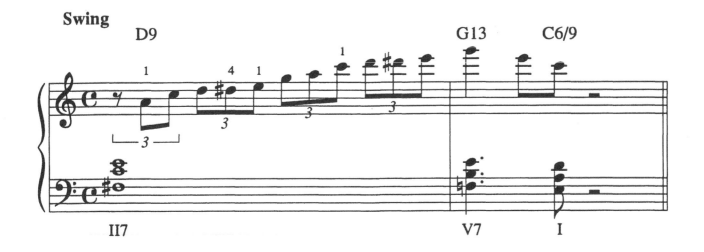

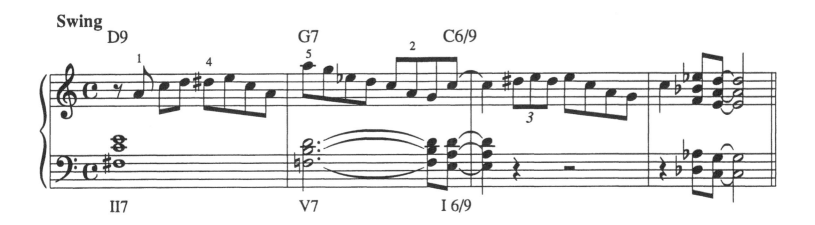

The C major blues scale with the VI7 chord:

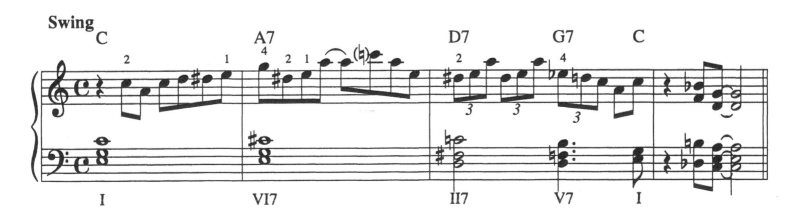

To summarize: in short phrases where the chord progression is I VIm7 IIm7 V7
or I VI7 II7 V7...the scale which complements the I chord may be
applied to the entire progression.

The parallel minor pentatonic scale and the major blues scale are almost identical. Compare:

C MAJOR BLUES SCALE   **C PARALLEL MINOR PENT. SCALE**

The P/m pent. scale emphasizes the ♭3. The combination of these two scales provides a basis for improvisation on the basic twelve measure blues chord progression. The major blues scale is played for the I and V7 chords and the P/m pent. scale is played for the IV7 chord. The major blues scale MAY NOT be played with the IV7 chord.

Below is a sample blues improvisation. The chords in measure two are optional.

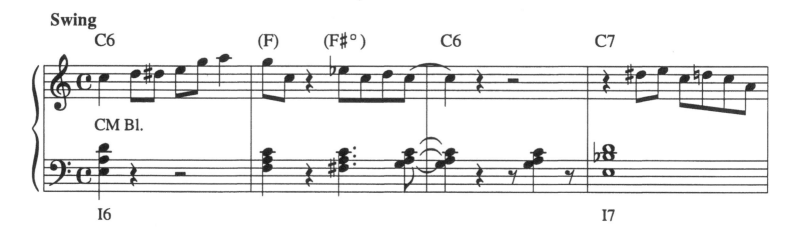

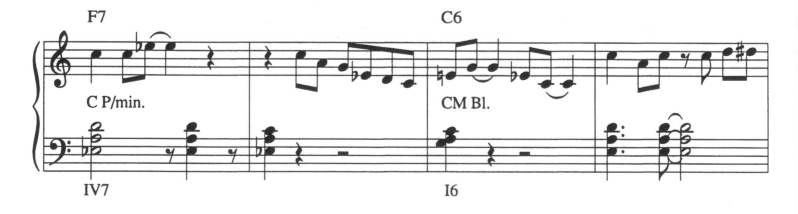

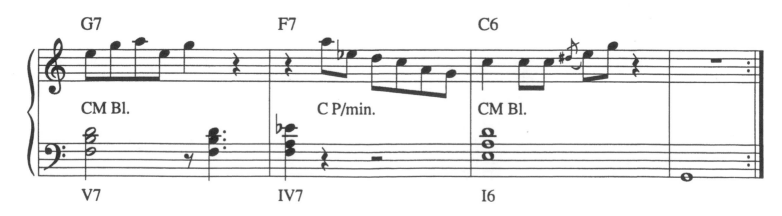

MAJOR BLUES SCALES

C

CHORDS: C6/9, C7, C9, C13

F

CHORDS: F6/9, F7, F9, F13

B♭

CHORDS: B♭6/9, B♭7, B♭9, B♭13

E♭

CHORDS: E♭6/9, E♭7, E♭9, E♭13

A♭

CHORDS: A♭6/9, A♭7, A♭9, A♭13

D♭

CHORDS: D♭6/9, D♭7, D♭9, D♭13

44

Gb

CHORDS: Gb6/9, Gb7, Gb9, Gb13

B

CHORDS: B6/9, B7, B9, B13

E

CHORDS: E6/9, E7, E9, E13

A

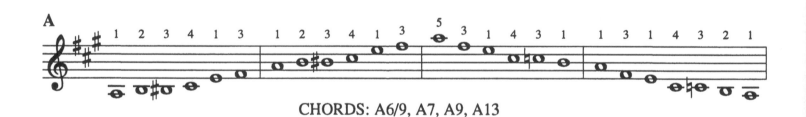

CHORDS: A6/9, A7, A9, A13

D

CHORDS: D6/9, D7, D9, D13

G

CHORDS: G6/9, G7, G9, G13

7: ADDING NOTES TO THE MAJOR BLUES SCALE

ADDING THE ♭7

The seventh note of the major scale is flatted and added to the major blues scale.

FORMULA: 1 2 #2 3 5 6 ♭7

C MAJOR BLUES SCALE WITH ♭7:

This scale in all keys appears at the end of the chapter.

APPLICATIONS:	Same as major blues scale except not good for endings.
CHORDS:	Dominant 7 9 13
RESTRICTIONS:	Same as major blues.

The entire scale may be played for fast fill-ins. For improvisation it is best to think major blues scale and occasionally add the ♭7 for effect. The addition of the ♭7 is especially good for blues improvisation.

The following drill could serve as a model for the practice of all scales. The right hand moves up and down the scale randomly usually not starting or ending on the tonic. The next scale begins on a note a step away from where the last scale ended. When linking one scale to another, a smoother connection results when the new scale begins on a note which is common to both scales. This common note method of linking scales is always possible when dominant seventh chord roots move by fourths as in the example.

Major blues scale with ♭7 DRILL:

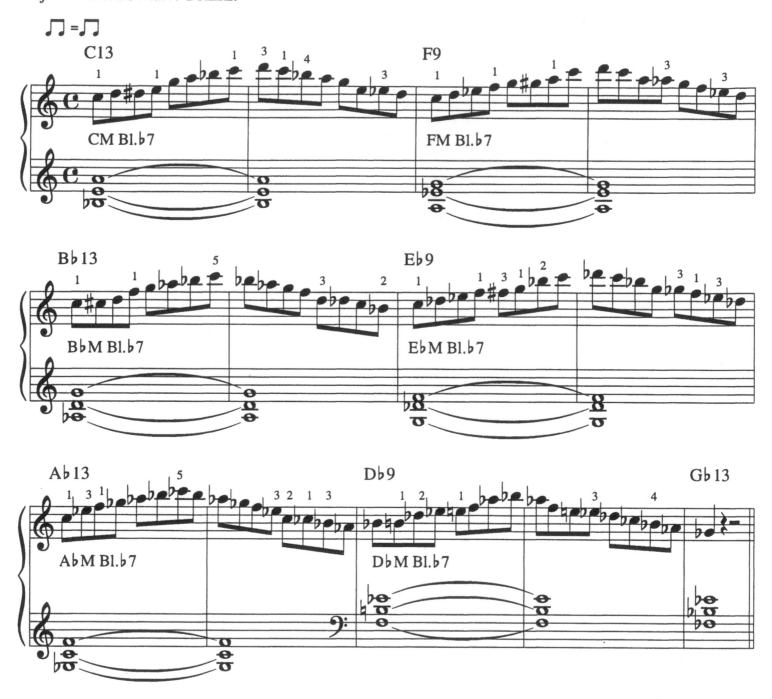

The dominant 7th chords move chromatically in the next example. Linking the scales by common tone is not practical in this type of chord movement.

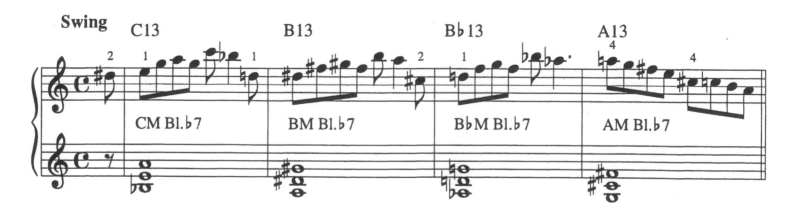

The 50's blues uses the ♭7. In this style a new scale is often selected for each chord change. The I, IV and V chords each take a scale whose tonic is the same as the chord root. In the next example the C chord is complemented by the C major blues scale with the ♭7 and the F and G chords with the F and G major blues with the ♭7.

ADDING THE ♯5 (♭6)

The fifth note of the major scale is sharped and added to the major blues scale. The resulting scale contains the natural fifth and the sharped fifth which is notated as a flatted sixth in descending passages.

FORMULA: 1 2 ♯2 3 5 ♯5 6

C MAJOR BLUES SCALE WITH ADDED ♯5 (♭6):

This scale in all keys appears at the end of the chapter.

APPLICATIONS:	Same as for the major blues scale. Excellent for fast Art Tatum-like fills and endings. Good for improvising.
CHORDS:	Same as major blues scale.
RESTRICTIONS:	Same as major blues scale.

The sharped fifth should be treated as a passing tone between the 5th and the 6th. When playing this scale, "pass through" the ♯5 (♭6) quickly. Do not end a phrase with or play a long note on this tone.

The following example is a series of IIm7 V7 progressions in several keys. The major pentatonic scales emphasize the 9th in the IIm7 chords. The major blues scale with the added ♯5 emphasizes the ♯5 in measures two and six. In measure four the ♯5 is treated as a passing tone.

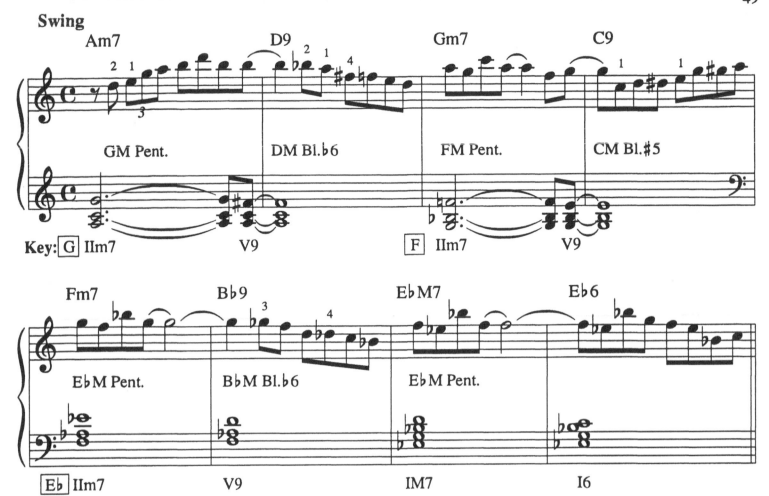

When the chords move every two beats all of the scale tones may not be present.

The major blues scale with the ♭6 as an ending in F major:

In practical playing several scales may be combined within an improvisation or fill-in. The melodic line may be constantly shifting from the major blues scale to the major blues with the ♯5 or ♭7 or the major pentatonic. Each scale has its own special characteristic and it is up to the keyboard player to determine which sound is desired at a particular point. The example below combines scales within the eight measures.

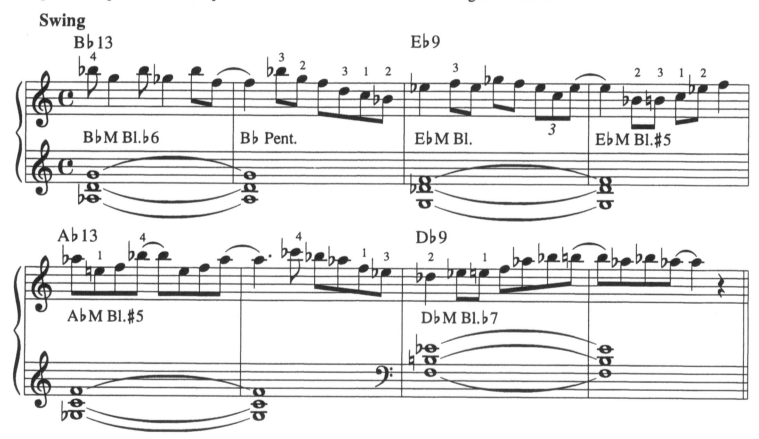

The major blues scale with the ♯5 works well with the I and V7 chords in the basic blues progression.

The scale will also complement the I VI7 II7 V7 progression discussed in the last chapter. In the next example the ♯2 and ♯5 are treated as passing tones.

MAJOR BLUES SCALES (add ♭7)

CHORDS: C7 9 13

CHORDS: F7 9 13

CHORDS: B♭7 9 13

CHORDS: E♭7 9 13

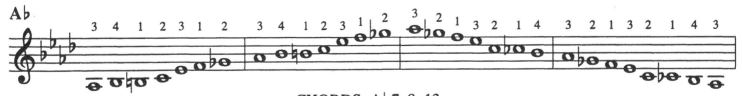

CHORDS: A♭7 9 13

CHORDS: D♭7 9 13

52

Gb

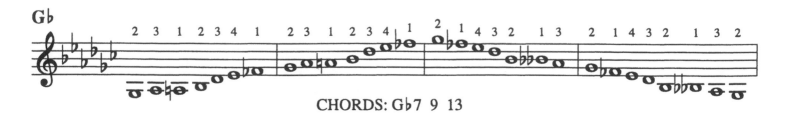

CHORDS: Gb7 9 13

B

CHORDS: B7 9 13

E

CHORDS: E7 9 13

A

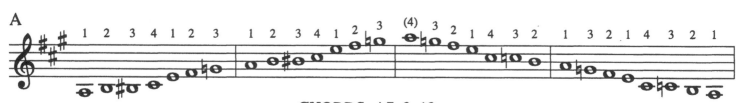

CHORDS: A7 9 13

D

CHORDS: D7 9 13

G

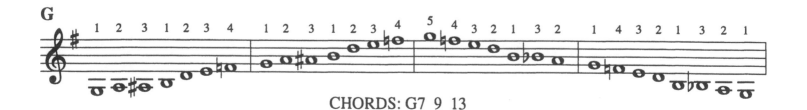

CHORDS: G7 9 13

MAJOR BLUES SCALES (add ♯5-♭6)

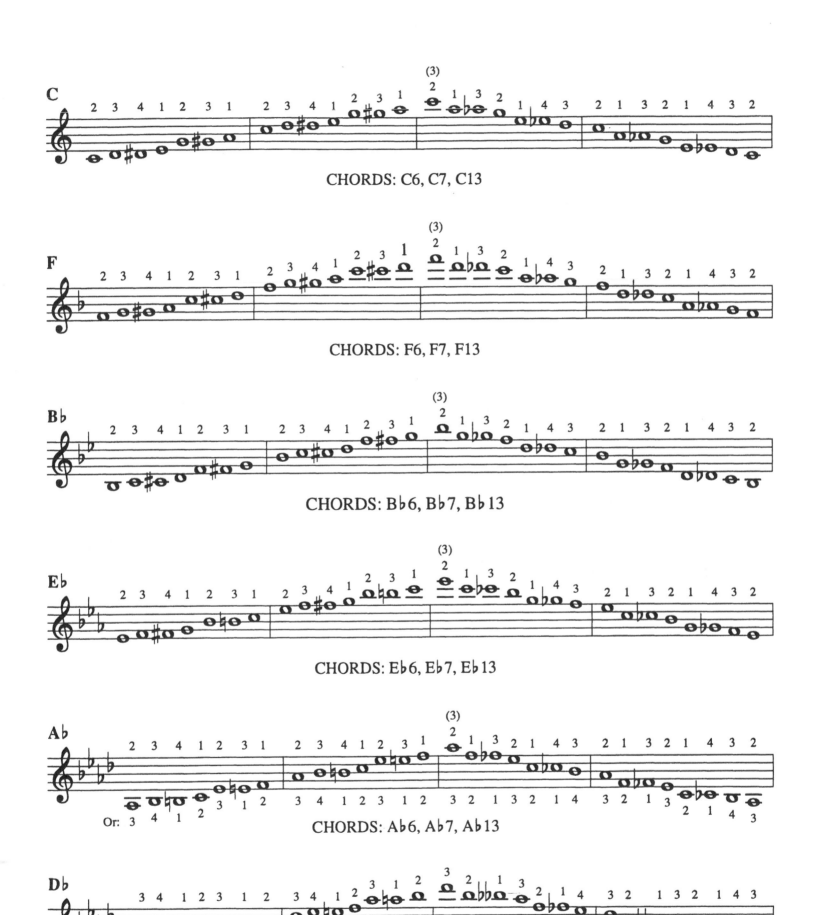

CHORDS: C6, C7, C13

CHORDS: F6, F7, F13

CHORDS: B♭6, B♭7, B♭13

CHORDS: E♭6, E♭7, E♭13

CHORDS: A♭6, A♭7, A♭13

CHORDS: D♭6, D♭7, D♭13

G♭

CHORDS: G♭6, G♭7, G♭13

B

CHORDS: B6, B7, B13

E

CHORDS: E6, E7, E13

A

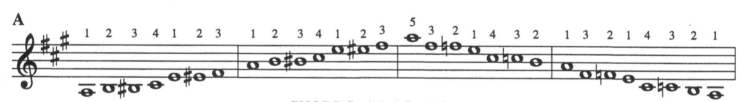

CHORDS: A6, A7, A13

D

CHORDS: D6, D7, D13

G

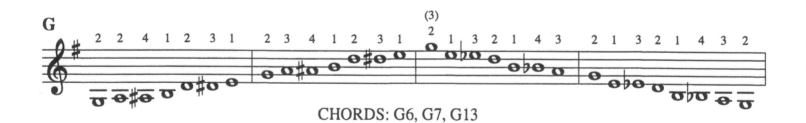

CHORDS: G6, G7, G13

8: THE MINOR BLUES SCALE

The minor blues scale is considered by many jazz theorists to be the only blues scale. This scale is another blues scale which produces a different effect or feeling. It is applied to blues and rock of the 70's and 80's and is also the primary improvising scale for a style called LATIN ROCK.

The major blues scale and the minor blues scale have the same relationship to one another as the traditional major scale has to its relative minor scale. The minor blues scale might be called the relative minor blues scale. Both scales contain the SAME NOTES. As in traditional harmony, the tonic of the minor blues scale is a minor third below the tonic of the major blues scale.

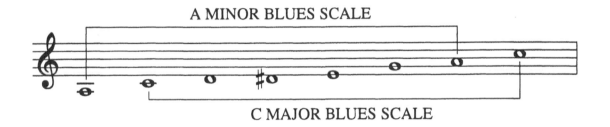

FORMULA: 1 ♭3 4 ♯4 (♭5) 5 ♭7 of any major scale

A MAJOR SCALE: **A MINOR BLUES SCALE:**

A MINOR BLUES SCALE:
(notated in the key of a minor)

This scale in all keys appears at the end of this chapter.

APPLICATIONS:	Major and minor key endings.
	Fast Tatum-like runs and fill-ins.
	Major and minor key improvisation.
	Blues and Latin rock.
CHORDS:	Dom. 7th functioning as I and IV in blues.
	Dom. 7th and m functioning as Im V7 minor key.
	m and dom. 7 functioning as Im IV7 Latin rock
	m7 m11
RESTRICTIONS:	V7 chords in major keys.

The ♭3 in the major blues scale produces the bluesy feeling. In the minor blues scale the ♭5 (♯4) serves this purpose.

The minor blues scale is sometimes played for endings on major key tunes.

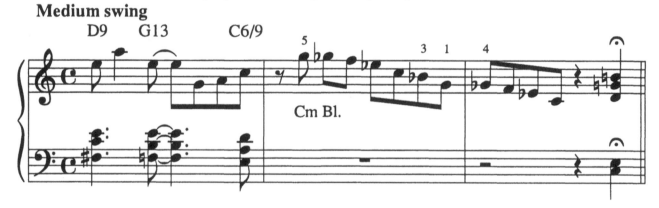

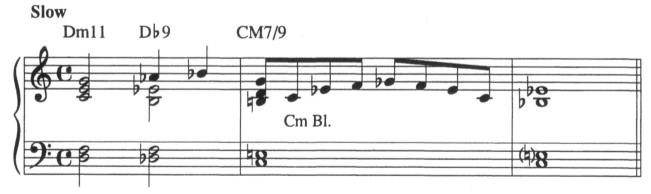

The next three exercises are in the keys of Am, Dm and Fm. The minor blues scale is applied to the Im and the V7 chords.

When the minor blues scale is played with the Im V7 in minor keys, the sound is similar to that of the minor pentatonic scale discussed in Chapter 3 (minor key improvisation). The two scales are identical and interchangeable except the minor blues scale contains the blues note (♭5). As with the major blues scale, the option is with the player as to how much to emphasize the blues note.

58

There are two types of minor key sounds or styles. The more traditional minor sound has the harmonic minor scale as its basis and contains the LEADING TONE. The leading tone is one half step below the tonic and is always the 7th in a major key. The ♭7 is one whole step below the tonic.

The scale numbers and formulae are based upon the major scale key signatures. However, as in traditional harmony, the minor blues scales are notated in the key signature of their relative major keys. (A minor notated in key of C major). In the example below the G♯ in the A harmonic minor scale is the leading tone 7th because the scale step numbers are derived from the A major key signature. In the A minor blues scale the G natural is the ♭7 (a flatted G♯ is a G natural).

A harmonic minor scale:

The more contemporary minor sound is based upon the minor blues scale and has no leading tone and emphasizes the ♭5 blues note.

A minor blues scale:

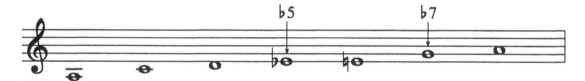

Examples A and B illustrate the difference in these two sounds. The key of A minor serves as the key for demonstration. Example A is traditional and B is contemporary. The scale choices are indicated in the music.

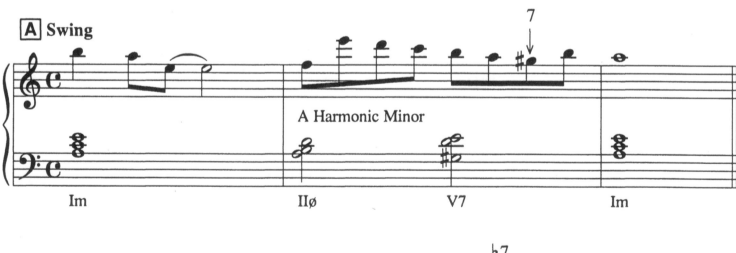

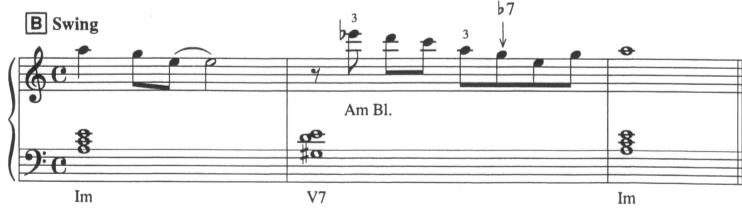

There are several scale choices for traditional minor. One is the harmonic minor which will not be discussed as it is a traditional scale and not within the scope of this book. Another is the parallel minor pentatonic scale. Example C applies the P/m pent. to the chord one half step above the V7 chord. This substitution was discussed in Chapters 4 and 5.

An additional variation allows the same scale which complements the ♭II9 to be played with the V7. Both chords work with this scale. Example C1 illustrates this point.

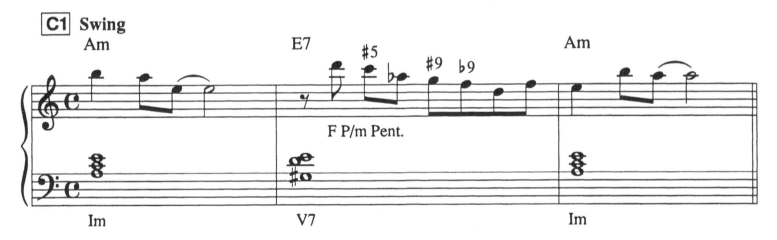

Yet another choice is available for the V7 chord in minor with a second parallel minor pentatonic. This scale in example D emphasizes the ♭9 in the V7 chord. The P/m pent. in example C1 emphasizes the ♯5, ♭9 and ♯9 in the V7 chord. These scales were discussed at the beginning of Chapter 5. The choice of scales is up to the player depending on which notes one wishes to emphasize.

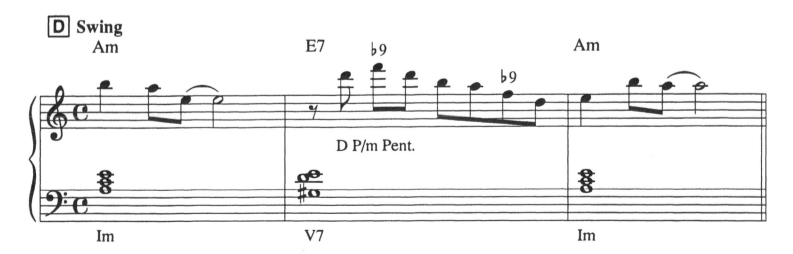

Examples E and F illustrate the P/m pent. scale mixed with the minor blues scale. The scale choice for the V7 chord emphasizes the #5, ♭9 and #9. This scale works well with both types of minor styles because it contains the leading tone and the ♭7th. (In this key the G# notated as an A♭ and the G natural.) Example E emphasizes the ♭7 and example F the leading tone 7th.

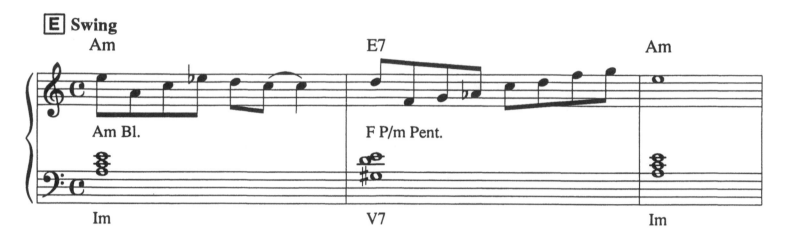

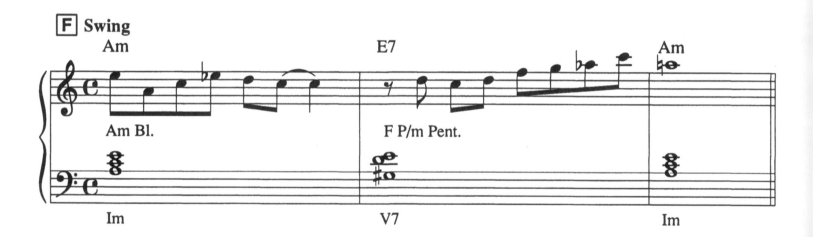

Play the preceding examples several times and HEAR the differences. The choice of scales is linked to style and eras in jazz. Many times the same scale may fit more than one historical jazz period.

The chord progression for many Latin rock tunes is Im7 IV7. Improvisations in this style are based on these two chords which are played over and over. The minor blues scale whose tonic is the same as the root of the Im chord is the basis for Latin rock improvisation. The following example is a Latin rock improvisation in the key of Gm. The chords are usually alternated a measure at a time. In measures 5 and 6 the chords alternate every two beats.

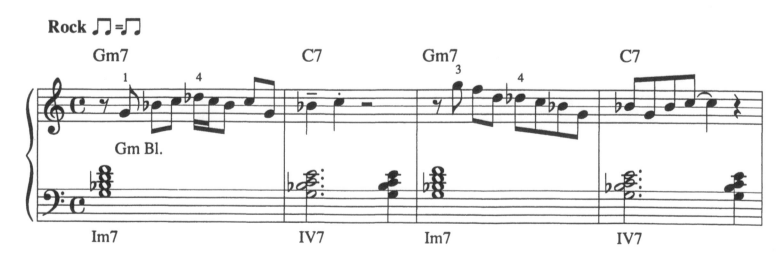

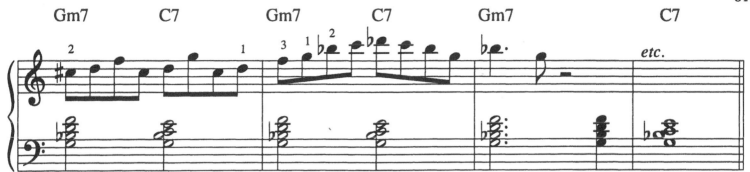

The minor blues scale will complement m7 and m11 chords regardless of their function. See the scale chart for specific chords and scales. The example below is a series of IIm7 V7 chord progressions. In this context the #4 is treated as a passing tone and the sound will not be bluesy unless this note is emphasized.

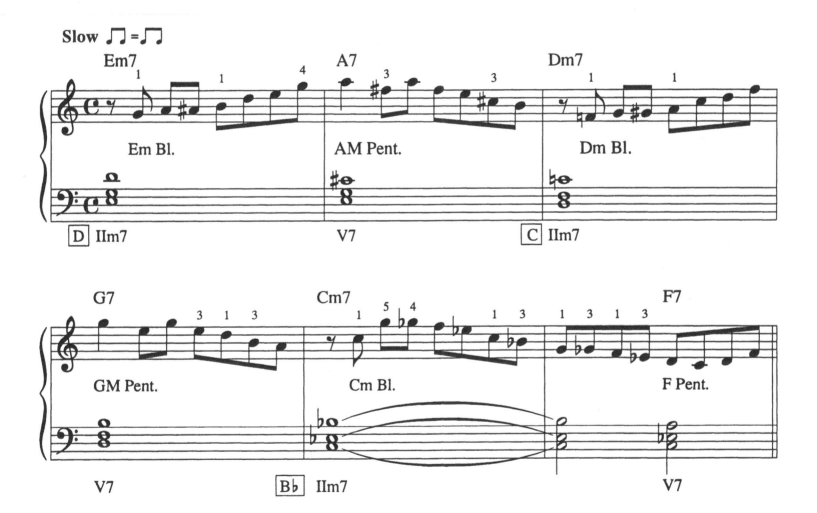

The minor blues scale is especially useful for blues improvisation. The scale whose tonic is the same as the root of the I chord may be played for the entire twelve measure progression.

Sometimes the major blues and minor blues scales are combined within a twelve measure improvisation. The minor blues scale is excellent with the IV7 chord. The next example represents the first eight measures of the blues progression. The major blues scale is played for the first four measures followed by the minor blues scale in measures 5 and 6 for the IV7 chord. Then there is a return to the major blues scale. The major blues scale should not be played with the IV7 chord.

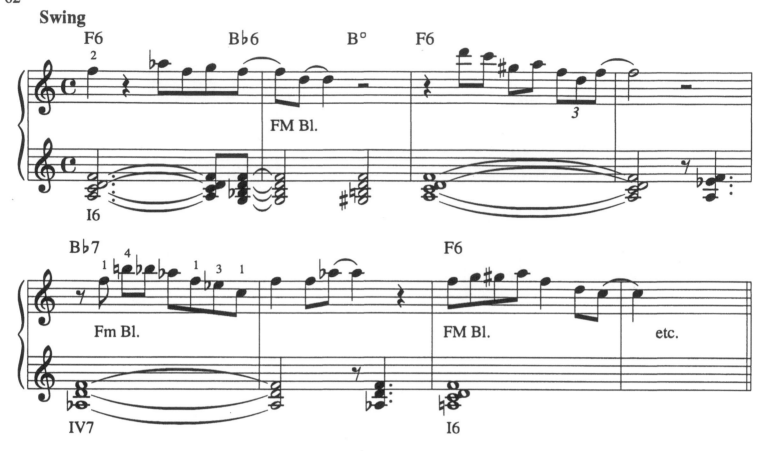

In more advanced situations, notes from one scale are BORROWED from another scale. The next example is a variation on the IV7 chord scale. The ♭7 is eliminated from the minor blues scale and replaced with the 6th borrowed from the major blues scale. The other minor blues scale notes remain the same. For the best effect precede this example with the first four measures of the last example.

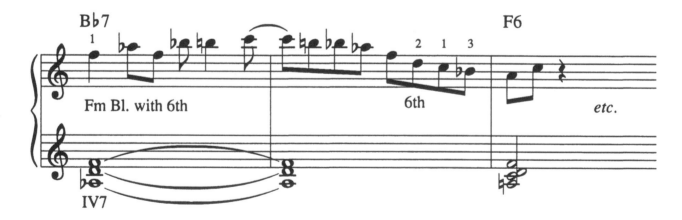

When the minor blues scale is applied to the I chord, the chord is often played as a I 7♯9.

The double note device as described in Chapter 3 (minor key improvisation) is effective with the minor blues scale. The scale notes or melody notes are on the bottom and the top note remains stationary. Two positions are necessary in order to include all scale tones.

F minor blues scale...double notes:

The examples below show the double notes with the I and IV7 chords. The chords are interchangeable. This device is played on only a few notes of a phrase and is not to be overdone.

MINOR BLUES SCALES

Am

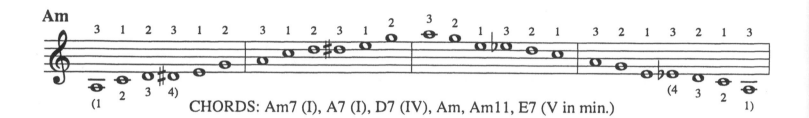

CHORDS: Am7 (I), A7 (I), D7 (IV), Am, Am11, E7 (V in min.)

Dm

CHORDS: Dm7 (I), D7 (I), G7 (IV), Dm, Dm11, A7 (V in min.)

Gm

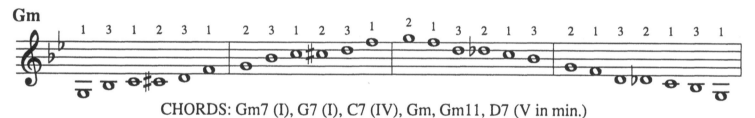

CHORDS: Gm7 (I), G7 (I), C7 (IV), Gm, Gm11, D7 (V in min.)

Cm

CHORDS: Cm7 (I), C7 (I), F7 (IV), Cm, Cm11, G7 (V in min.)

Fm

CHORDS: Fm7 (I), F7 (I), B♭7 (IV), Fm, Fm11, C7 (V in min.)

B♭m

CHORDS: B♭m7 (I), B♭7 (I), E♭7 (IV), B♭m, B♭m11, F7 (V in min.)

E♭m

CHORDS: E♭m7 (I), E♭7 (I), A♭7 (IV), E♭m, E♭m11, B♭7 (V in min.)

G♯m (A♭m)

CHORDS: A♭m7 (I), A♭7 (I), D♭7 (IV), A♭m, A♭m11, E♭7 (V in min.)

C♯m (D♭m)

CHORDS: D♭m7 (I), D♭7 (I), G♭7 (IV), D♭m, D♭m11, A♭7 (V in min.)

F♯m (G♭m)

CHORDS: G♭m7 (I), G♭7 (I), B7 (IV), G♭m, G♭m11, D♭7 (V in min.)

Bm

CHORDS: Bm7 (I), B7 (I), E7 (IV), Bm, Bm11, F♯7 (V in min.)

Em

CHORDS: Em7 (I), E7 (I), A7 (IV), Em, Em11, B7 (V in min.)

9: THE MINOR BLUES SCALE WITH ADDED 7

The 7th (leading tone) may be added to the minor blues scale. This note is the same tone as the #5 in the relative major blues scale. Therefore the relationship between the major blues and the minor blues scale whose tonic is a minor third below remains the same. Both contain the same notes even with the added notes. The 7th is written as a flat 1 in descending passages.

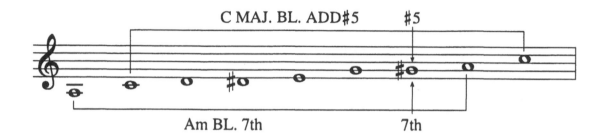

FORMULA: 1 ♭3 4 #4 (♭5) 5 ♭7 7 of any major scale.

A MINOR BLUES SCALE ADD 7:

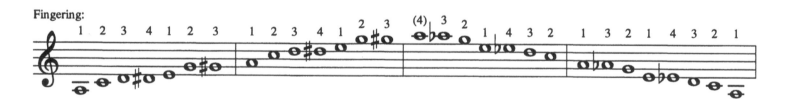

This scale appears in all keys at the end of this chapter.

APPLICATIONS:	Same as minor blues scale.
CHORDS:	Same as minor blues scale...except not good for IV7 in blues.
RESTRICTIONS:	Limited use...follow principles set forth in this chapter.

This scale contains both the ♭7 and the leading tone 7th and is therefore compatible with both types of minor feelings discussed in the previous chapter. The added note is most effective in fast continuous runs descending or ascending. When improvising in slower tempi it is best to think minor blues scale and occasionally add the 7th.

The example below illustrates a fast run as an ending to a slow song in an ad lib tempo.

The next two examples are improvisations in the keys of Dm and Fm.

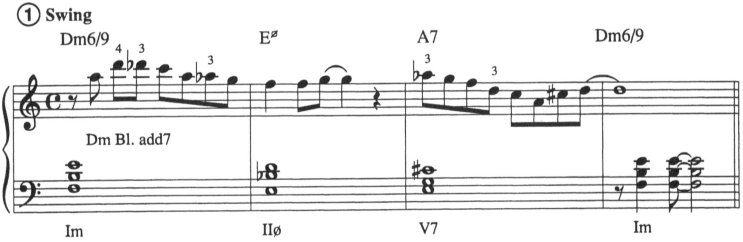

The minor blues add 7 may be applied to m7 chords in the IIm7 V7 chord progression in major keys. In this context it is best to treat the ♭5 and 7th as passing tones or as chromatic approaches to adjacent scale tones. The approach should be from below and not above.

The descending scale will introduce a slight bluesy effect. The choice as to how to treat the 7th and the ♭5 is up to the player. Below is a series of IIm7 V7 chord progressions.

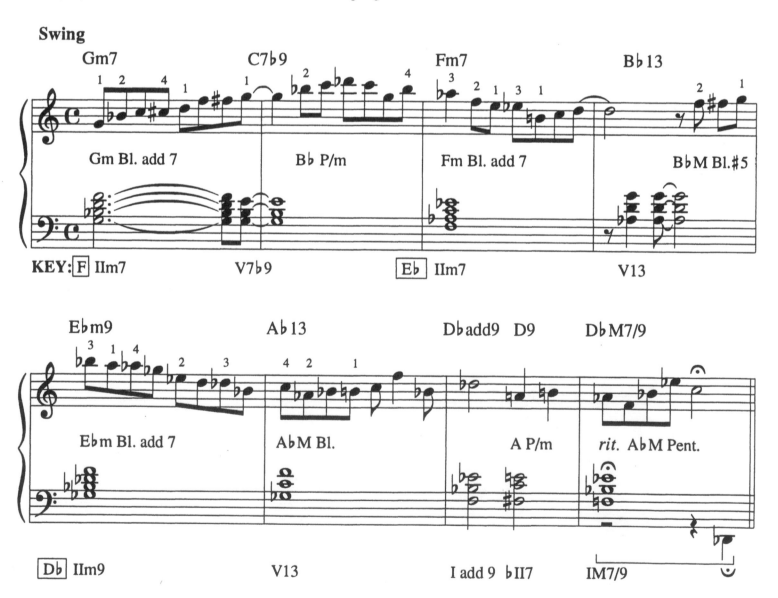

In Latin rock the added 7th should be treated as a chromatic passing tone. Study the next example.

Latin rock improvisation:
Scale: Gm Bl. add7

The added 7th must be applied sparingly to the blues. Unless the line moves rapidly through the added note, trouble will result! Experiment and make a choice. The minor blues scale with the added 7th WILL NOT WORK with the IV7 chord. Stick to the minor blues or try other options discussed in previous chapters.

The minor blues scale is strong enough to stand alone. The added 7th must be dealt with carefully in all styles of jazz. When in doubt...don't play it!

SUMMARY OF SCALE USE FOR BASIC BLUES

CHORDS	SCALES					
	MAJOR BLUES	MAJ. BL. add ♭6	MAJ. BL. add ♭7	MINOR BLUES	MIN. BL. add 7	P/m Pent.
I 6/9	●	●				●
I7	●	●	●			●
I7♯9				●	●	
IV7				●		●
V7	●	●		●	●	●

SUMMARY OF BLUES SCALE USE

CHORDS	SCALES				
	MAJOR BLUES	MAJ. BL. add ♭6	MAJ. BL. add ♭7	MINOR BLUES	MIN. BL. add 7
6/9	●	●			
m				●	●
m7, m11				●	●
Dom. 7 9 13	●	●	●		
Dom. 7 (IV)				●	
Dom. 7 (V7 min.)				●	●

MINOR BLUES SCALE ADD 7

Am

CHORDS: Am7 (I), A7 (I), Am, Am11

Dm

CHORDS: Dm7 (I), D7 (I), Dm, Dm11

Gm

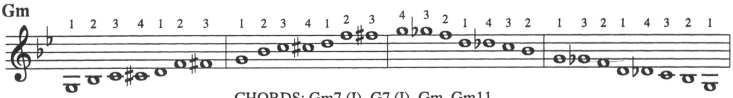

CHORDS: Gm7 (I), G7 (I), Gm, Gm11

Cm

CHORDS: Cm7 (I), C7 (I), Cm, Cm11

Fm

CHORDS: Fm (I), F7 (I), Fm, Fm11

B♭m

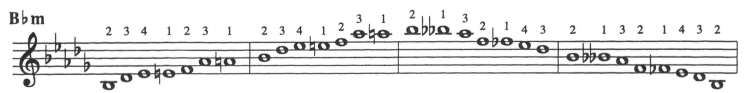

CHORDS: B♭m7 (I), B♭7 (I), B♭m, B♭m11

72

E♭m

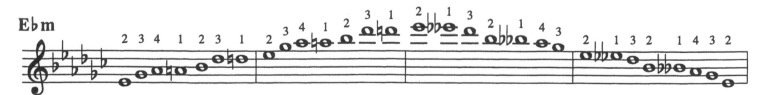

CHORDS: E♭m7 (I), E♭7 (I), E♭m, E♭m11

G♯m (A♭m)

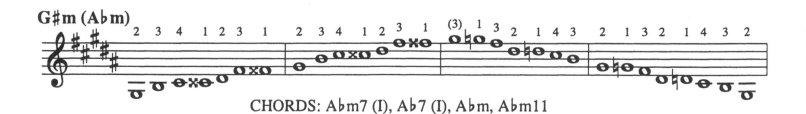

CHORDS: A♭m7 (I), A♭7 (I), A♭m, A♭m11

C♯m (D♭m)

CHORDS: D♭m7 (I), D♭7 (I), D♭m, D♭m11

F♯m (G♭m)

CHORDS: G♭m7 (I), G♭7 (I), G♭m, G♭m11

Bm

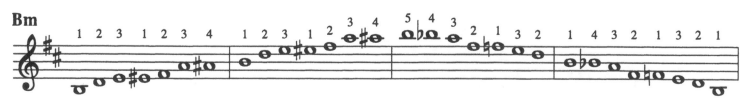

CHORDS: Bm7 (I), B7 (I), Bm, Bm11

Em

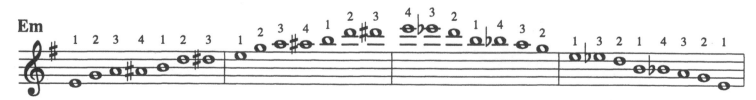

CHORDS: Em7 (I), E7 (I), Em, Em11

10: PUTTING IT ALL TOGETHER

In practical playing, chords sometimes change more frequently than once per measure. It is therefore not possible to include all scale tones in an improvisation or fill-in. When chords and scales change rapidly link the scales together by common tone or start the new scale on a note close by.

Below is a common chord progression with the chords and scales changing every two beats. Notice that the notes do not always follow the sequence of the scale.

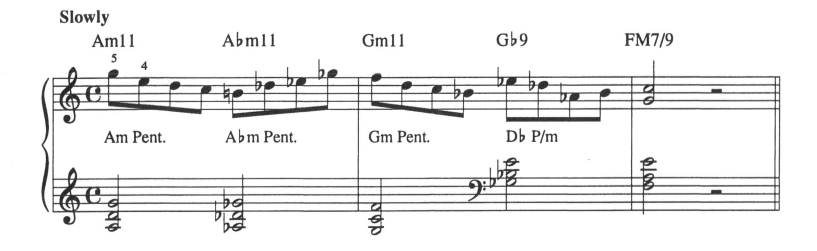

The following is another example of linking scales together every two beats. The progression is a series of random major seventh chords.

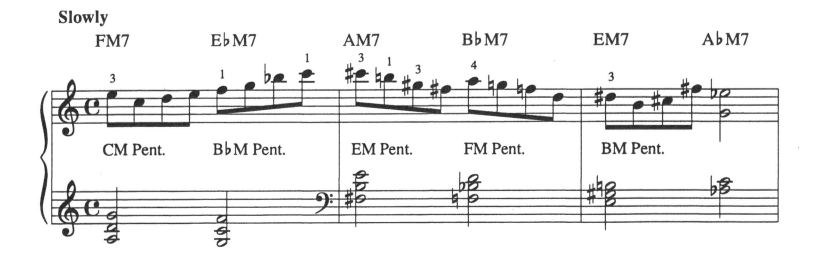

FINDING CHORD/SCALE RELATIONSHIPS

It is a simple matter to find any chord/scale relationship.

PROBLEM: To find the chord/scale relationship for Aø.

1. Refer to the summary chord/scale charts below and on the next page. There are two choices for the ø chord. Select one.

2. Turn to the chapter dealing with this scale and check at the beginning to see if there are any functional restrictions.

3. Turn to the scale charts at the end of the chapter and find which scale complements the Aø.

ANSWER: C P/m or FM Pent. add ♭7

SUMMARY OF PENTATONIC SCALE USE *

CHORDS	SCALES			
	MAJOR PENT.	MINOR PENT.	MAJOR PENT ♭7	PARALLEL MINOR
6/9, M7	●			
M7#11	●			●
m7, m11		●		
m9	●			
ø			●	●
m6				●
Dom.7 9-13	●		●	●
Dom.7♭9				●
Dom.7 ♭9 #5 #9				●
V7 (natural min.)		●		●
Dom.7 sus	●			

* See Appendix

SUMMARY OF BLUES SCALE USE *

	SCALES				
CHORDS	MAJOR BLUES	MAJ. BL. add ♭6	MAJ.BL. add ♭7	MINOR BLUES	MIN. BL. add 7
6/9	●	●			
m				●	●
m7, m11				●	●
Dom. 7 9 13	●	●	●		
Dom.7 (IV)				●	
Dom.7 (V7 min.)				●	●

SUMMARY OF SCALE USE FOR BASIC BLUES *

	SCALES					
CHORDS	MAJOR BLUES	MAJ. BL. add ♭6	MAJ. BL. add ♭7	MINOR BLUES	MIN. BL. add 7	P/m Pent.
I 6/9	●	●				●
I 7	●	●	●			●
I 7♯9				●	●	
IV 7				●		●
V 7	●	●		●	●	●

* See Appendix

The next example reflects a Dixieland style.

Most of the scales discussed in this book are applied to the following chord progression and are linked together to form a jazz improvisation. Study the example carefully with an awareness of which scales are played with which chords and how they are linked together. Notice the key changes.

Over the years literally hundreds of different blues chord progressions have evolved from the original I IV7 V7. Musicians are constantly striving to seek new substitution chords for the blues. The next example is a blues with several substitute chords. Play and analyze the example.

Mod. fast (in 2)

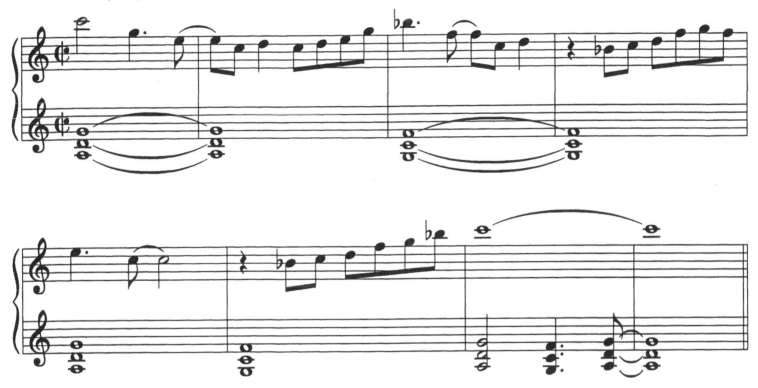

It must be stressed once again that the so called "jazz" scales presented in this volume are not meant to be played exclusively for fill-ins or improvisations. Traditional major and minor scales, modal scales and broken chords (arpeggios) are a vital part of improvisations and fill-ins. It is the combination of all these devices which produces a good jazz line.

Always be aware of the style of the music. Choose the scale which fits the style. The context of the chord progression influences the style. The major pentatonic scales applied to a series of dominant ninth chords sounds like the swing style of the 40's. The same major pentatonic scales applied to the series of random major seventh chords in this chapter suggest a style altogether different.

The purpose of this book is to explore and to recognize the potential of the jazz scales. If the keyboard player is able to find a way to include some of these scales in practical playing situations, the study of this book will have been worthwhile.

APPENDIX

Below are the scale/chord relationship charts which appear on pages 74-75. In this example SPECIFIC chords and scales are indicated. Chord/scale relationships in all keys may be found by transposing this chart.

SUMMARY OF PENTATONIC SCALE USE

CHORDS	SCALES			
	MAJOR PENT.	MINOR PENT	MAJOR PENT ♭7	PARALLEL MINOR
C6/9	C			
CM7/9	G			
CM7♯11	D			A
Cm7 11		C		
Cm9	B♭			
Cø			A♭	E♭
Cm6				C
C 7 9 13	C		C	G
C7♭9				B♭
C ♭9 ♯5 ♯9				D♭
C7 (min.)		F		B♭, D♭
C7 sus	B♭			

SUMMARY OF BLUES SCALE USE

CHORDS	SCALES				
	MAJOR BLUES	MAJ. BL. add ♭6	MAJ. BL. add ♭7	MINOR BLUES	MIN. BL. add 7
C6/9	C	C			
Cm				C	C
Cm11				C	C
C 7 9 13	C	C	C		
C7 (IV)				G	
C7 (V in min.)				F	F

SUMMARY OF SCALE USE FOR BASIC BLUES

CHORDS	SCALES					
	MAJOR BLUES	MAJ. BL. add ♭6	MAJ. BL. add ♭7	MINOR BLUES	MIN. BL. add 7	P/m PENT.
C6/9 (I)	C	C				C
C7 (I)	C	C	C			C
C7♯9 (I)				C	C	
C7 (IV)				G	G	G
C7 (V)	F	F		F	F	F